TABLE OF CONTENTS

DISCLAIMER AND TERMS OF USE AGREEMENT:

Introduction – There is something interesting about employers in today's economy…

Chapter 1 – Setting Yourself Up As A Freelancer

Chapter 2 – Defining Your Specialty

Chapter 3 – Niche-By-Niche Profits

Chapter 4 – Book Publishing Rocks!

Chapter 5 – Survival Planning is a Huge Niche

Chapter 6 – Forensic Science and Catching Cyber-Criminals

Chapter 7 – Advice & How To Information Products

Chapter 8 – Miscellaneous Niches That Rock!

I Have a Special Gift for My Readers

Meet the Author

Employees Are Out - Freelancers Are In
How to Work from Home as an Independent Freelancer
©Copyright 2013 by Dr. Leland Benton

DISCLAIMER AND TERMS OF USE AGREEMENT:

(Please Read This Before Using This Book)

This information is for educational and informational purposes only. The content is not intended to be a substitute for any professional advice, diagnosis, or treatment.

The author and publisher of this book and the accompanying materials have used their best efforts in preparing this book.

The author and publisher make no representation or warranties with respect to the accuracy, applicability, fitness, or completeness of the contents of this book. The information contained in this book is strictly for educational purposes. Therefore, if you wish to apply ideas contained in this book, you are taking full responsibility for your actions.

The author and publisher disclaim any warranties (express or implied), merchantability, or fitness for any particular purpose. The author and publisher shall in no event be held liable to any party for any direct, indirect, punitive, special, incidental or other consequential damages arising directly or indirectly from any use of this material, which is provided "as is", and without warranties. As always, the advice of a competent legal, tax, accounting, medical or other professional should be sought where applicable.

The author and publisher do not warrant the performance, effectiveness or applicability of any sites listed or linked to in this book. All links are for information purposes only and are not warranted for content, accuracy or any other implied or explicit purpose. No part of this may be copied, or changed in any format, or used in any way other than what is outlined within this course under any circumstances. Violators will be prosecuted.

This book is © Copyrighted by ePubWealth.com.

Introduction – There is something interesting about employers in today's economy…

Yes, there is something very interesting about employers in today's economy. When the economic downturn hit in 2008, companies began downsizing just to stay alive. They furloughed and laid off or fired a good many employees and by doing this, they placed the job duties of the departing workers squarely on the backs of employees that remained aboard.

But then something really interesting began occurring late in 2012 and 2013. Economic conditions improved and these very same companies began making money again but guess what? These very same companies began to realize that they DID NOT NEED the employees that they had released and so they were never hired back.

If that isn't a hit and a half on everybody's' butt then I don't know what is! They stayed alive by releasing employees and placing the departing job duties on the employees that remained but then as their balance sheets improved, they ignored the employees they had released and continued to expect the existing employees that were not laid off to continue doing multiple jobs. AMAZING!

And you wonder why the unions got so big!!!

This book understands the current employment trends and the need for people to earn a living. It will teach and describe in detail how to become an independent freelancer and work from home by accessing a ton of resources I give you in this book.

Recently I published a book by my sister, Nancy Benton on "Getting Paid For Everything You Do!!" which went over the top sales-wise to best-selling status in just a few days...

It provides resource links to literally hundreds of websites where you can make money. Then one of my associates, Dr. Noah Pranksky published a book, "How To Retire Without Money," which also went over the top sales-wise too and became a best-selling book in just a few days:

Both these books are appropriate for the subject matter we will be discussing. I was the adviser on both books so I know what they contain and I highly recommend you buy both of them and use them in conjunction with this book.

You can find these books by going online to the ePubWealth.com Library Catalog:
EPW Library Catalog Online

http://www.epubwealth.com/wp-content/uploads/2013/07/Leland-benton-private-turbo.pdf

EPW Library Catalog Download
http://www.filefactory.com/f/562ef3ea1a054f0a

The primary goal and purpose of this book is to demonstrate to my readers that there is life after being laid off and after this economic recession goes by and these factors just may have done you a big favor as I show you how to become an independent freelancer while working from home.

I have been working from home since 1989 when the web became available to the general public and loving it but it is not for everybody. Some people just cannot work from home with all of the distractions; they just can't seem to say no to Oprah and the refrigerator.

It is important to realize that working from home has tremendous advantages but also some downsides you need to consider.

I like the fact that I rarely use my car and no longer have to pay for upkeep and maintenance. I can't remember when I last went to the dry cleaners, and my insurance rates and gas bills have dropped too. I can work in total privacy and no longer have to get dressed in a suit and tie. In fact my work attire is usually shorts and a tank top. I am connected to my office by computer and most of my workers are freelance independent contractors that I assign tasks to and pay per task completed.

So let's begin. Throughout the pages of this book I am going to show you "niches" of freelancing task that have been super profitable to me but first I will begin by teaching you how to set yourself up as a freelancer.

Chapter 1 – Setting Yourself Up As A Freelancer

First we need to set you up as a freelancer and then I will identify websites where you can go and find jobs.

Next, I will teach you how to define your specialty by accessing the things you have a passion for is the easiest way to become a freelancer

I will then take you niche-by-niche on freelancing opportunities that have been super profitable for me.

To begin, you can operate as a sole proprietor using your social security number as your tax I.D. You can file a **fictitious business name** statement known also as a DBA or "doing business as" with your local city clerk.

Take this DBA statement to your bank and open a **business checking account** under your DBA name.

BIG NOTE: This is very important!!! As a freelancer you are paid gross wages. You must **file a quarterly estimate tax form** with the IRS to remain legal. Please consult a bookkeeper or CPA for more information. My accountant does this for me. I send him an Excel spreadsheet every quarter of the money I have made and he files my estimate tax form quarterly. **DO NOT FORGET TO DO THIS!!!** You do not want any problems with the IRS and you cannot go the entire year and then file with your gross wages. DON'T DO THIS!

As your freelance business grows, you can begin consider forming a **limited liability corporation or LLC**. Mine is filed in the state of Nevada and this is the best place to form an LLC. You can either do it yourself by downloading the LLC forms from the Nevada Secretary of State website or hire a Nevada Incorporator to do it for you.

http://nvsos.gov/index.aspx?page=428

Next is a **business license** filed where you reside. Just go to your county website and look for the county clerk and/or business license heading depending on how large a city you live in.

You need to also consider **business insurance**. Consult an insurance agent about insuring your home office – this is available whether you own your home or rent. I have added to my home owner policy my home office. I also have business general liability insurance. Since working from home has become so popular, many insurance companies are offering general liability insurance in SMP or small multiperil plans or packages that do it all under one policy. Ask a local insurance agent.

This is optional but you may want to consider a **company logo, business cards, and brochures,** depending on what niches you are working. I use a graphic artist overseas and she is great and inexpensive. Sanchita Dutta: solution.bn@gmail.com

Just write to her with what you need. I use her for **book covers, logos, favicons for my websites, banners, website headers and footers,** just about everything because she is a full service graphics designer and she knows her stuff.

Okay, with all of the above accomplished, you are now legally a freelancer.

Next, you need to outline exactly the tasks you can do and want to do. In other words, do you want to specialize in any one job? You don't have to decide now; finish reading this book and the other ones cited in the introduction before you decide.

We will get more into defining your specialty in Chapter 2.

Once you decide on your specialty or the tasks you want to do, here are some sites where you can post the jobs you want and bid on jobs posted:

Freelance
http://www.agentsofvalue.com/
http://www.daydreamservices.com/
https://www.elance.com/
http://www.freelancer.com/

http://www.freelancers.net/
http://www.guru.com/
http://www.myzoox.com/
https://www.odesk.com/
http://www.peopleperhour.com/
http://www.skillwho.com/
http://workaholics4hire.com/
http://taskrabbit.com
http://microworkers.com

It is going to be tedious at first setting yourself up on all of the sites listed above but remember you only need to do it once.

This is important: Do not load yourself up with jobs where you cannot deliver the work on time. This will affect your freelance record and you do not want poor ratings. Also, deliver more than the customer expects so they write you fabulous reviews.

Always have a backup computer to fall back on if your computer takes a dump. If you can afford it just buy a laptop at Cosco, BestBuy or Walmart. You can use this until you get your computer fixed.

You will want to always invest in yourself by buying programs that make your repetitive jobs easier. For example, I have hundreds of logins and passwords so I use Roboform to keep track of them all and then log me in automatically. Go here for Roboform:

http://www.roboform.com/php/pums/rfprepay.php?affid=ta556

Do not forget to back up your computer daily. I use Dropbox to keep all of my stuff backed up but I also backup to an external hard drive daily.

https://db.tt/ngaCTyxN

This is also important: there are two aspects to freelancing. One is what I am describing in this book – becoming a freelancer and doing jobs for other people. The second is where you hire other freelancers to do jobs for you by posting jobs in the sites I have provided above. I do both!!!

Okay, once you have accomplished all of the above, you now a legal freelancer and ready to take on work and get paid.

Let's now discuss defining your specialty…

Chapter 2 – Defining Your Specialty

Candidly, this is where the rubber meets the road. It is important to define the jobs/tasks that you are willing to perform and then bid on these jobs by building an **online reputation** as a freelancer that is good and trustworthy. Your online freelancer reputation will make or break your level of income. As I said previously, always deliver more than the customer expects.

I want to re-emphasize that you **don't want to take on more than you can handle**. There are literally thousands of jobs online that are available to do but don't become a "kid in a candy shop" and load yourself up with tasks where you fail to deliver on time.

Another good tip is to **set a schedule** where you work your freelance jobs. You can easily become a freelance junky working long hours where your social life suffers as well as your health. I have visited freelance friend in the evening after the dinner hour and they were still in their pajamas and hadn't even showered or shaved. Don't do this!! Set a schedule and develop good freelance habits from the start.

Furthermore, it is quite easy for you to fall into the habit of snacking or eating fast foods in lieu of **proper nutrition**. Again do not so this!! Set a time to prepare normal and healthy meals so that your health is not affected.

Next, set some time to get **AWAY FROM THE COMPUTER**. Even if it is just a visit to your local Starbucks for a cup of coffee or to run errands, you need to get away from your computer and recharge your batteries.

Okay, in my freelance business I pretty much center around jobs that I have a passion for; specifically, book writing and publishing, survival planning, forensic science, cooking and baking, advice & how to informational products.

I will define each one in the upcoming chapters and then I will show you a bunch of really profitable niches where you can make gobs of money.

Defining your specialty using what you are passionate about is the smart way to go because if you have a passion for the subject, doing task for it will be fun.

Personally, I hate repetitive tasks. They drive me nuts so I will farm these tasks out to other freelancers.

Okay now that you are legally a freelancer and you are considering your specialty; let's move on to defining profitable niches for you….

Chapter 3 – Niche-By-Niche Profits

There are literally tons of niches you can select from and below is just a partial list:

Airline Tickets
Apartment Seekers
Astrology
Auto Insurance
Auto Loans
Automobiles
Business News
Business Opportunities
Cars Listing Services
Celebrity Gossip
Computers and Technology
Coupons
Credit Card Seekers
Debt Leads
Ebay
Education

Employment
Entertainment
Entrepreneurs
Ethnic
Event Seekers
Fashion
Financial Services
Franchises
Freebies
Gamers
Golf
Health
Hollywood
Home
Horoscope Related
Insurance
Internet Based Earning
Investors
Loans
Lottery
Movies
NASCAR
Netscape
Networking-Business
Networking-Dating
Networking-Social
Networking-Woman
News
Parents
Photography
Real Estate
Shopping
Sports

Stocks Investment
Travel
Trend Setters
Weather
Weight Loss

Here is an article I think you will enjoy…

Finding and Filling Book Marketing Niches
Posted Sun, 05/23/2010 - 16:58 by Bob Spear

http://www.publetariat.com/book-trends/finding-and-filling-book-marketing-niches

I have been a niche marketer all my adult life. For me, niche filling and creativity go hand in hand.

In college, I created the only rock and roll band with multiple horns on the Indiana University campus. In the 1980s, I created a society orchestra with a sound similar to "Big Bad Voodoo Daddy," before they ever came on the scene and played all the formal dances at Ft. Leavenworth and later on the Bavarian Fest Circuit out of Munich, Germany for three years. From 1987 to 1997, I became the go-to- author for military self-defense and personal security books. Now, my wife and I are doing it again at our bookstore, The Book Barn, and with my publishing company, Spear's Mint Editions Publishing. For me, finding a niche and filling it is as natural as breathing. I have always had an instinct for it. I'm not rich, but I've had a lot of fun along the way. I would like to use my store and writing/publishing efforts over the past ten years or so to explain what and how we do what we do.

Heads Up—Look Around
It's important to be aware—sensitive to patterns in life and the day-to-day routines. What do people like, want, and need? Are they being satisfied? Are any fads becoming trends (a genuine turning point)? What excites and interests you and the people you service? Listen to what people say. Watch the news. Talk; get opinions. Watch and experience life. Here is how all that works:

The American Girls product line came out. What a great idea—hooking American history to female characters representing different periods and producing common formats to each one. We decided that was a good idea and began to organize events around single characters at a time. Instead of holding tea and doll admiration parties, we created a full context experience. We would pick a character and invite customers with girls 6-11 years old for an hour-long experience. I would quickly explain the historical period for the chosen character. I would play and sing a couple of songs from that time and culture. We would play a game from that time. Then came a short craft or art project centered on the time, after which we served a typical snack from the time. The little girls loved it and the parents could be heard commenting in the background, "I didn't know that." These events helped us receive a win in a national level competition amongst many other Independent bookstores.

Leavenworth was the first city in Kansas and has a rich historical background. We have always had a good regional selection of books. In 2000, I decided to add music to that by creating a CD album of ten songs—5 were original songs I wrote to tell fun stories about our area and 5 were traditional folk songs that had connectivity to our area. It has sold slowly but steadily ever since.

Next we noticed we had no attractive book below $15 for the tourists about our community. There were some excellent histories, but they were hardbacks in the $50 to $60 price range. They were fine for interested locals, but not for casual tourist shoppers. I asked several area historians if they would be interested in writing such a book, and they weren't. So, I took it on and spent six months researching and writing in 2005 to produce Leavenworth: First City of Kansas. This book won three marketing awards for its cover and interior design and has sold steadily with lots of favorable feedback. Four area museums and several gift shops sell it and the CD, as well as our store.

Don't Be Surprised if You Earn A Reputation As A Reliable Resource—That's What You Want to Happen

An interesting phenomenon has occurred. People are now introducing me as an area historian. My choosing to expand my storytelling programs into the next higher level called historical performing, where I become the famous Leavenworth favorite son, William F. (Buffalo Bill) Cody. I tell his stories in the first person, as if I really was him. I try to make him come alive for the listeners. Now, my college degrees are in music and business. I've had one American history course and four music history courses in my time. That does not make me a professional historian; however, the research I have done to put together credible projects and events provide me with enough knowledge to be interesting.

Now I am taking this Leavenworth/Midwestern history niche and adding something that has been missing—a body of literature that provides a clear picture of pop culture of our area's frontier times. My last post was a review of a wonderful book that explained how to find and re-publish public domain materials. What a Godsend that was! I have been able to locate a number of nonfiction and fiction books of the 1800s to early 1900s that opens wonderful windows of the exciting era. How much have I had to invest? Mostly my time and skills and very little money. I have downloaded text or html files, pasted them into Word format, and then used InDesign to lay out the books with an old-timey look. The covers are simple black ink printed on colored card stock.

Now I have a unique offering in our niche. Could competitors do this? It's doubtful; it's too skill dependent and too small of a market segment for the big box stores, and there are no Indy stores in the area with the ability to pull it off. This is the ultimate example of "Long-Tail" marketing—find little niches that need filling but are too small for the big guys. Next week I will have ten copies of each of these digitally printed to provide enough for the store and to show the other outlets. See what I mean about not having to make a large investment. I will then use just in time inventory control to drive future print runs. Since I don't have to use middlemen for these books, I can afford the higher pod costs. So, what are these long-lost tomes that will catapult our store's image several notches upward? They are a good mix of nonfiction and fiction and an amalgamation of the two:

The Prairie Traveler— *In 1859 an Army Captain who spent 25 years guiding settlers across the plains safely write the ultimate how-to book on doing this. He addresses the animals you'd need and why, the equipment, the supplies, and the skills. He also provides the day by day mileposts along all the major trails. This is an absolutely fascinating book, even providing information on the major Indian tribes you might encounter and what to expect.*

Twin Hells— *Leavenworth has a prison industry—7 of them in the area. This 1800s book was written by a man who founded one of our banks and was also president of an insurance company in Atchison. Political competitors managed to railroad him into an 18-month sentence on a trumped up fraud charge to the Kansas State Penitentiary, working in its very dangerous coal mine. After serving his time, he is hired as an investigator of Missouri's penitentiary, which he finds to be just as bad. He takes his notes in shorthand so the guards won't know what he's writing about. There will be a lot of interest in this book in our unique community.*

Adventures of Buffalo Bill From Boyhood to Manhood— *Deeds of Daring, Scenes of Thrilling Peril, and Romantic Incidents in the Early Life of W.F. Cody, the Monarch of Bordermen. By Colonel Prentiss Ingraham, who was a master of pulp fiction. The subtitle* *is straight off the book's title page. Buffalo Bill is of huge interest here.*

There are several, but I think you'll get the idea by these illustrations.

Emerging Pop Book Trends
Next, I noticed that novels of "place" had become popular. Setting is important to people. My wife also noticed the trend of adults buying Young Adult books for their own reading pleasure because they want entertaining, easy and quick to read books. That combination of factors is what prompted me to write and publish a series of five simple mysteries set in Leavenworth with easy-to-recognize settings and archtypical Leavenworth characters. People love them.

Niche-Filling Creates Credibility and Trust
Notice all these projects and events are supportive of our community. We continue to raise the public's awareness of our store and ourselves as a trustworthy source of information and entertainment based on the community past and present. This brings in more foot traffic of people interested in the niche and all our other offerings. They simply cannot get this kind of support at a major chain. We know the area; we know our books; we know the authors (many of them personally), and we know how to fit it all together with an additional service of fast, reliable special ordering of book not on our shelves. By approaching our niche from several different directions with different product types, I hope this gives you an idea of the mindset that you should find useful in this essential marketing attitude in today's marketplace.

Beginning in the next chapter I will go into detail on the niches I concentrate and do.

Chapter 4 – Book Publishing Rocks!

To begin, I want to first introduce you to two very special words – PASSIVE INCOME!! Passive income is income you earn 24/7, day-after-day, month-after-month, even while you sleep where you first set it up and then there is no further involvement on your part; it is income that continues to pour in.

Writing books – authorship – and publishing books is one of the most lucrative passive income opportunities on the planet.

There are literally almost a hundred main publishing platforms available to self-publishing indie authors. But out of these hundred, there are six major publishing platforms where you can publish your books and in turn they will put them up on the various platforms listed. Here they are;

Kindle Direct Publishing – Owned by Amazon, this is the largest self-publishing platform on the net today. Amazon also owns CreateSpace: http://kdp.amazon.com/

Createspace - Standard: Amazon.com, Amazon Europe, Createspace Store. Expanded: Bookstores and Online Retailers, Libraries and Academic Institutions, Createspace Direct independent bookstores and book resellers: https://www.createspace.com/

Smashwords - Apple iBookstore, Barnes & Noble, Sony, Kobo, Diesel, Baker & Taylor:
http://www.smashwords.com/

Lulu.com - Amazon .com US, UK, France, Germany, Italy, and Spain stores, $75 Ingram Catalog retailers Amazon.com, BN.com, local bookstores, etc, iBookstore:
http://www.lulu.com

BookBaby - iBookstore, Amazon Kindle, Barnes and Noble PubIt, Sony eReader Store, Kobo, Copia, Gardner Books, Baker & Taylor Bookstore, eBook Pie, eSentral:
http://www.bookbaby.com/

BookLocker - Amazon.com, BarnesandNoble.com PubIt, BooksaMillion.com and many other smaller, online bookstores, both domestic and foreign. Any bookstore with an Ingram account can pick up Ingram's feed. http://publishing.booklocker.com/

Now many of you may not be able to write a sentence but this doesn't matter. In my best-selling book, "How To Write a Kindle Book in Hours," I explain the different ways that you can write books without having the talent of being a writer yourself.

You can find the book by going online to the ePubWealth.com Library Catalog:
EPW Library Catalog Online
http://www.epubwealth.com/wp-content/uploads/2013/07/Leland-benton-private-turbo.pdf

EPW Library Catalog Download
http://www.filefactory.com/f/562ef3ea1a054f0a

I offer free webinars that teach people everything they need to know about the self-publishing business. Go here and download the free webinar recordings as well as all the goodies I give away.

Webinar Download Portals
http://tinyurl.com/epubwebinar
http://tinyurl.com/epubwebinar2
http://tinyurl.com/epubwebinar3

I also offer an advanced class for people who require one-on-one instruction. Go here for more details:

http://www.epubwealth.com/epubwealth-advanced-program/

Everything I teach is part of my ePublishing series of book:

Copyright Law Guidebook – Learning the ins-outs of copyright law is easy with this guidebook. It contains everything that authors should be aware of and incorporate into their manuscripts.

How to Promote Your Book Online & Offline – writing a book is part of it; advertising, marketing and promotion is the other part. Learn how to pulse your book to best-selling status with this book.

How To Promote Your Book Online & Offline Vol 2 – More book promotion and marketing techniques to assist in your book sales.

How to Write a Kindle Book in Hours – Don't be left out of the self-publishing indie author craze. Even if you cannot write a single word, this book will show you how to cash in on book publishing

How to Write Compelling Content – Content is king and keeps your readers coming back for more. Learn how to write compelling content with this book.

International Standard Book Numbers – ISBNs are important and are required by all of the publishing platforms. Learn all about ISBNs in this book and learn to do it right the first time.

Promoting Your Video Book Trailers – Promoting your books on YouTube and the hundreds of free video sharing site increases your book sales exponentially. This book teaches you how to do videos as well as provides subcontractors to do it for you.

Publish with a Purpose – Ghostwriting can be super profitable. Learn how to become a ghostwriter and how to write books for business owners at the same time. Once you purchase this book, the download portal will also provide you with a sample video book trailer and sample legal agreement to use to contract your services with clients.

The ePubWealth Program – this is the basic authoring course which describes how to write books and the publishing platforms that sell them for you.

The ePubWealth Program ADVANCED – This is one of the most advanced book writing and marketing courses on the net today with over $10,000 in downloads available once you sign up.

The Publishing Agreement – if you use a publishing house to publish your books then you need to know about publishing agreements.

You can find these books by going online to the ePubWealth.com Library Catalog:
EPW Library Catalog Online
http://www.epubwealth.com/wp-content/uploads/2013/07/Leland-benton-private-turbo.pdf

EPW Library Catalog Download
http://www.filefactory.com/f/562ef3ea1a054f0a

Currently I personally have over 200-books published on the Amazon Kindle platform alone and it isn't even my most profitable platform. Smashwords is my most profitable platform, then Lulu.com and third is Amazon kindle. On all three platforms I am making a healthy five figure monthly income from each platform…do the math.

On Kindle I make a 70% royalty on all my books sold; book writing and publishing is lucrative.

Can you do this? Yes, you can and with my one-on-one instruction, I can get you to best-selling author status quickly. Like I said, even if you cannot string words together to form a single sentence, I can show you how to cash in on book publishing.

Without a doubt this is one of the best if not "THE" best forms of passive income. Please consider this opportunity carefully.

Authors are important. Without authors the world would be ignorant. We entertain, we cajole, we teach and we make a difference. The world still holds authors in high esteem and rightly so because authors change the way we think, the way we live and the way we live our lives. My email inbox is stuffed daily from readers and their success stories and I engage my readers because they are important to me. Without my readers, my words fall to the ground and mean nothing.

Becoming an author means that you are making a difference in other people's lives. My passions translate into more than just income. The results of my work are evident from the emails I receive from my readers. I wouldn't give up being an author if you put a gun to my head. It is without a doubt the most rewarding of my career paths.

Authorship involves so many avenues of opportunities I literally cannot list them all here but my books on ePublishing above speaks about most of them. I will touch on one that is very lucrative...Ghostwriting.

As described above, my book "Publish with a Purpose," describes the ghostwriting opportunity in detail.

In this chapter I want to touch on some of the bullet points that make this a huge moneymaker. However; with that said, ghostwriting is not a passive income opportunity. You simply charge a fee to your customer who wants a book written but published under their own name as author.

Ghostwriting can be super profitable. Learn how to become a ghostwriter and how to write books for business owners at the same time. Once you purchase the "Publish with a Purpose" book, the download portal will also provide you with a sample video book trailer and sample legal agreement to use to contract your services with clients.

As a best-selling author, I command a high price for books that I ghostwrite. I charge anywhere from $997 to $5,000 per book with the average price being $2500 depending on the book, its content, length, etc. and it usually takes an average of about 30-days to complete

Who pays ghostwriters to ghostwrite books?

By far, the largest source of customers is business owners that use the books as business cards. Authors hold a certain amount of prestige amongst the general public and the service provider industry – lawyers, consultants, real estate agents and brokers, etc – are always contracting with me to ghostwrite their books. They use the books I write for them as justification that they are experts in their field and also use them as a kind of "business status symbol".

Once you begin ghostwriting, it quickly brings in customers by word-of mouth and you are not required to do any heavy advertising and or promotional work.

Here is a list of freelance sites where you can list your services and get job orders:

Freelance
http://www.agentsofvalue.com/
http://www.daydreamservices.com/
https://www.elance.com/
http://www.freelancer.com/
http://www.freelancers.net/
http://www.guru.com/
http://www.myzoox.com/
https://www.odesk.com/
http://www.peopleperhour.com/
http://www.skillwho.com/
http://workaholics4hire.com/

Once you have your book or a ghostwritten book published you will need to promote it. Here is a list of top promo sites:

Let These Sites Know 7+ Days Before Your Promo Starts

It's important to plan ahead your marketing for your free promotion. This list of sites requires 7+ days notice of your promo in order to post it.

http://www.pixelofink.com/sfkb/
http://bargainebookhunter.com/contact-us/
http://www.thatbookplace.com/free-promo-submissions/
http://indiebookoftheday.com/authors/free-on-kindle-listing/
http://www.freebookdude.com/p/list-your-free-book.html
http://the-cheap.net/authors/free-promotion-opportunities/share-your-deal/
http://awesomegang.com/submit-your-book/
http://www.fkbooksandtips.com/for-authors/
http://thefrugalereader.wufoo.com/forms/frugal-freebie-submissions/
http://ebookshabit.com/for-authors/
http://www.freebookshub.com/authors/
http://www.ebooksfreedaily.com/?page_id=16
http://ebooklister.net/submit.php
http://www.centsibleereads.com/p/for-authors.html
https://docs.google.com/spreadsheet/viewform?formkey=dHI3UVVZdTZkWUo3d2w3aDExbXk5MEE6MQ#gid=0
http://www.frugal-freebies.com/p/submit-freebie.html
http://onehundredfreebooks.com/contact.html
https://docs.google.com/spreadsheet/viewform?formkey=dFpBd0JUMk9KZzZ0TXJBYXRENFZYMVE6MQ

Fiction Sites
http://freekindlefiction.blogspot.com/p/tell-us-about-free-books.html
http://www.freebooksy.com/editorial-submissions

http://www.kindlemojo.com/contact-info/
http://www.centsibleereads.com/p/for-authors.html

Post On These Sites The Day Your Promo Starts Or 24 Hours Before
http://snickslist.com/books/place-ad/
http://www.freebookclub.org/kindle-books/book-submissions/
http://addictedtoebooks.com/free
http://www.daily-free-ebooks.com/suggest-free-ebook
http://www.ereaderiq.com/contact/

Free Book Twitter Influencers
These Twitter users all have medium to large followings on Twitter who love to hear about free books.
@freebookclub1
@ibdbookoftheday
@Booksontheknob
@bookbub
@kindle_free
@freeebooksdaily
@kindlefreebooks
@zilchebooks
@freedailybooks
@free2kindle
@freereadfeed
@pixelofink
@digitalinktoday
@fkbt
@kindlestuff
@free_kindle_fic
@Bookyrnextread
@CheapKindleDly

@DigitalBkToday
@kindlenews
@ebook
@freeebookdeal
@free
@free_kindle
@freebookdude
@4FreeKindleBook
@FreeKindleStuff
@IndAuthorSucess
@IndieKindle
@kindleebooks
@KindleBookKing
@KindleFreeBook
@KindleUpdates
@Kindle_promo
@KindleDaily
@WLCPromotions

UK Twitter Users:
@free_uk_ebooks

Facebook Groups For Authors
These are all great groups to join on Facebook to network and connect with other authors, share marketing ideas, ask questions and build relationships. I highly recommend you join these groups if you're a serious author!

https://www.facebook.com/groups/KindlePublishers/
https://www.facebook.com/groups/kindleauthors/
https://www.facebook.com/groups/357112331027292/
https://www.facebook.com/groups/bookmarketing/
https://www.facebook.com/groups/512098985483106/

https://www.facebook.com/groups/291645554239114/
https://www.facebook.com/groups/apablog/
https://www.facebook.com/groups/204725947524/
https://www.facebook.com/groups/204968026218845/
https://www.facebook.com/groups/2204546223/
https://www.facebook.com/groups/179494068820033/
https://www.facebook.com/groups/borntowrite/
https://www.facebook.com/groups/6092061939/
https://www.facebook.com/groups/135486133130440/
https://www.facebook.com/groups/110604178950149/

Facebook Groups For Fiction Authors
https://www.facebook.com/groups/fiction.nonfiction/
https://www.facebook.com/groups/174995555883415/
https://www.facebook.com/groups/2207480509/
https://www.facebook.com/groups/fanfictionlookout/

Facebook Groups For Promoting Your Free Books
https://www.facebook.com/groups/270558336379692/
https://www.facebook.com/groups/126278657527255/
https://www.facebook.com/groups/freebkrus/
https://www.facebook.com/groups/FreeTodayOnAmazon/
https://www.facebook.com/groups/215918835174776/
https://www.facebook.com/groups/1013820968756497/
https://www.facebook.com/groups/426282137432533/
https://www.facebook.com/groups/freeebooks/
https://www.facebook.com/groups/341840249197060/
https://www.facebook.com/groups/182637088529255/
https://www.facebook.com/groups/294455560643884/
https://www.facebook.com/groups/370900356880/
https://www.facebook.com/groups/236927589749427/

Personally, I am very heavily involved in book promotion and my free webinars explain some of the best techniques I use. But by far, invest in my following books to get the best understanding of how to sell books online and offline.

How to Promote Your Book Online & Offline

How To Promote Your Book Online & Offline Vol 2

How To Promote Your Book Online & Offline Vol 3

Promoting Your Video Book Trailers

How To Create, Market & Sell Audiobooks

How To Create, Market & Sell Videobooks

You can find these books by going online to the ePubWealth.com Library Catalog:
EPW Library Catalog Online
http://www.epubwealth.com/wp-content/uploads/2013/07/Leland-benton-private-turbo.pdf

EPW Library Catalog Download
http://www.filefactory.com/f/562ef3ea1a054f0a

To date, I am responsible for thousands of people becoming authors and making big money online and they too enjoy the passive income while they continue to write and increase their book inventories.

Without a doubt, authorship and self-publishing offers the best passive income sources, ghostwriting can be accomplished in conjunction with an author's other activities.

You can become a ghostwriter or you can hire a ghostwriter to write your books. The majority of ghostwriters do not command my high fees because they are NOT best-selling authors. The average fee a ghostwriter charges for a 50-page book is $120. Most ebooks are 40-50 pages.

Chapter 5 – Survival Planning is a Huge Niche

I am very big on this subject and I make no qualms about it. The operative word here is PLANNING. My corporate motto is "Be prepared to Survive!"

I have written extensively on this subject with most of my books skyrocketing to best-selling status within just a few days:

Be a Prepper
PrepperNations Blueprint
Be Prepared to Survive
SurvivalNations Catalog
SurvivalNations - Surviving a Disease Pandemic
Surviving A Financial Crisis
Surviving YOU
The Truth About Federal Anti-Hoarding Laws

You can find these books by going online to the ePubWealth.com Library Catalog:
EPW Library Catalog Online
http://www.epubwealth.com/wp-content/uploads/2013/07/Leland-benton-private-turbo.pdf

EPW Library Catalog Download
http://www.filefactory.com/f/562ef3ea1a054f0a

Let me tell you how I got into this segment of business. I was in Las Vegas shopping with my girlfriend at the Fashion Show Mall. She was trying on clothes and doing what women do when shopping when suddenly she came running out to tell me she thought the changing room mirror was a two-way mirror. I had taught her how to check the mirrors to see if they were two-way so I went in and verified, yes it was a two-way mirror. I went up to the sales clerk and asked her to call thee manager. When the manager arrived, I demonstrated that his store had two-way mirrors in the dressing rooms. He informed me and my girlfriend that it was necessary to cut down on shoplifting. I informed him that it was illegal to have two-way mirrors in the dressing rooms even if he posted it on the outside of each dressing room, which it wasn't.

I then called the police and filed a report for voyeurism. Next I filed a lawsuit against the store, which was quickly settled out of court. My girlfriend and I returned to this store months later and the two-way mirrors had been removed. This is why survival planning and privacy issues are both big topics with me.

In my book PrepperNations Blueprint, I describe how I began forming neighborhood survival groups and providing my neighbors with survival products. This wasn't about selling products; the selling part was the effect; the cause was providing a needed service to my community. The concept literally took off with people emailing me how to duplicate what I was doing in their neighborhoods nationwide. All of this activity came from publishing my book PrepperNations Blueprint.

From this one book I wrote a survival checklist book called "Be Prepared to Survive" and it offered a complete checklist of what to consider in survival planning so nothing was left out. Along with this book I published a survival catalog of products that I personally use and could vouch for call SurvivalNations catalog.

Be Prepared to Survive
SurvivalNations Catalog

Just last week from writing this I published "SurvivalNations - Surviving a Disease Pandemic," which also skyrocketed to best-selling status in just a few days.

SurvivalNations - Surviving a Disease Pandemic

My point is this: this is a topic that is on a good many people's minds. Think about it, the evening news is full of natural disasters from hurricanes to tsunamis, earthquakes to volcanic eruptions. And if Mother Nature isn't enough, the evening news is full of the assault on our schools and children, mass murders, child predators, white slavery, and more. Everywhere we turn some disaster and or crisis is rearing its ugly head.

Then we have government that can't get their act together. There is no bi-partisanship, no agreement on anything. The 2012 elections were a joke; the fact that the country is broke doesn't seem to bother anybody as government spending continues to spin out of control. And then you have the European Union coming apart at the seams. There is rioting in Greece and Spain over austerity measures. Italy is just about ready to blow up and more.

Last but not least, you have the results of the Arab spring uprisings in 2012 with Egypt, Tunisia, Libya and now Syria throwing off the dictator yokes and replacing them with what? More dictators? Yep! With all of what I said above, is survival planning necessary? You betcha! And what is the central core of your existence…your HOME!

Chapter 6 – Forensic Science and Catching Cyber-Criminals

Think about it; cyber crime is going out of sight as the economy worsens. Here is an article from the New York Times to demonstrate just how weird things are getting…

Editorial
Sneaky Apps That Track Cellphones
Published: December 23, 2012

http://www.nytimes.com/2012/12/24/opinion/sneaking-after-cellphone-users.html?nl=todaysheadlines&emc=edit_th_20121224&_r=0

A perversion of smartphone technology called "stalking apps" — precise, secretive tracking of the movements of cellphone users — is increasingly a matter of national concern, particularly for domestic abuse victims. No less threatening is the routine monitoring of children's locales and phone habits for commercial purposes while parents are kept in the dark. Stealth apps even stoop to cyber-leering through the now notorious app called Girls Around Me, which allows men to search out women, unbeknown to them, by cross-matching GPS technology with information and photo sites like Facebook.

With these abuses proliferating, the Senate Judiciary Committee this month took a big step to protect the privacy of all cellphone users and close legal loopholes that enable stalking apps. The committee approved a worthy measure sponsored by Senator Al Franken, Democrat of Minnesota that for the first time would require cellphone companies to obtain a user's permission to collect location data and sell it or share it with third parties. It also would flatly outlaw creation of stalking apps, applying criminal and civil penalties.

"Right now companies — some legitimate, some sleazy — are collecting yours or your child's location and selling it to ad companies or who knows who else," Mr. Franken told the committee. He described a constituent who was not aware that her spouse had secretly installed an app on her phone to stalk her movements — and send her text threats along the way — as she went to court for a protection order. It takes mere seconds, the senator said, for an abuser to slip a stalking app into another person's phone. The need to protect children was echoed in a recent Federal Trade Commission study showing that some of the most popular apps for children engage in

commercial phone stalking, with no notification to parents.

Current laws banning stalking and wiretapping lag behind modern communications, with no provision barring companies from marketing a stalking app. One company sells such an app for about $50, and advertised on its site: "Suspect your spouse is cheating? Don't break the bank by hiring a private investigator."

The measure is opposed by software companies, which say they can police themselves. This is highly unlikely considering the money to be made by this lucrative and fast-moving technology. The Senate should approve the measure and move it for House action with speed worthy of the Internet.

*****

I am very big in forensic science and privacy issues because I see the damage being done daily to companies and people from hackers and crackers. As big as my ForensicsNation unit is – 22,000 cyber forensics investigators in 22-counties, WE DON'T EVEN MAKE A DENT in cyber-crime. I write the software that catches to bad guys online. Cyber-criminals have no idea how we track them down and nab the.

What I have put together form y readers is a program where it teaches you to track down cyber-criminals and turn them in to law enforcement and collect the reward. It is called the ForensicsNation Bushwhacker Program.

Everything in this program is done from home. You never see or confront the cyber-criminal. There are hundreds of 'wanted" websites on the net that list the cyber-criminal and the reward. Using the program outlined above, you can easily find and track cyber-criminals. If they own a cellphone, laptop, tablet and are online YOU OWN THEM.

The FNC Bushwhacker Program also teaches you how to protect you and your loved ones too.

Let me give you an example of ways to make money. I charge $497 to scan a cell phone for spyware planted on it and remove it if found. Ex-wife, ex-husbands and tons of other perpetrators are constantly planting spyware on cell phones for nefarious reasons. In any given week I scan and clean 25-30 cellphones. Do the math!!

Here is another moneymaker. I offer a service that scans a residence or business for hidden cameras and listening devices. I charge $497 for this service. With the new wireless technology, cameras are as small as a button and can transmit what it see wirelessly over the internet. I get more requests for services form college students than any other customer and I usually find hidden cameras spying on them too. Flipping weird!!!!

I had one customer – she was a waitress for the restaurant chain Hooters – call me and when I scanned outside her bedroom window, I found a wireless camera in a tree and it was in the process of transmitting so I track the signal down the street to find a guy in a car with a handheld viewing device. You should have seen his face when the cops surrounded his car and yanked him out of the vehicle. He is now serving five years for voyeurism.

People, it never ends. There is so much business out there you simply can't get to all of it or train personnel to handle it.

The opportunities are endless in the forensics business. As a forensics investigator your job is to track the dirtbag down, compile and preserve the evidence. YOU ARE NOT A PEACE OFFICER and you do not have arresting authority so you never confront the dirtbag; you call in law enforcement to do the bust.

You are not a private investigator and you do no field work whatsoever. The services I cited above are not investigative field work. You are not tracking anybody; you are simply providing a service. Hence you do not need any special licensing.

When you become an amateur internet sleuth – bushwhacker- you will find an interesting thing that develops. You begin to "specialize" in certain internet crime. I have bushwhackers that specialize in identity theft, spyware, cyber stalkers, and more. I, myself, specialize in child predators and child abusers because it is one of my passions as you can tell from the books I write on the subject and more:

Confessions of a Child Predator
Child Watch
Cyber-Daters Beware
Cyber Protect Your Business

ForensicsNation Bushwhacker Program
ForensicsNationsStore.com Catalog
Protecting Yourself from Cyber Crime
Stealing You
Was Sandy Hook a Hoax?
Why Women Should Not Use Online Dating Services
You Can Run But You Cannot Hide

You can find these books by going online to the ePubWealth.com Library Catalog:
EPW Library Catalog Online
http://www.epubwealth.com/wp-content/uploads/2013/07/Leland-benton-private-turbo.pdf

EPW Library Catalog Download
http://www.filefactory.com/f/562ef3ea1a054f0a

Yes, you can become a bushwhacker and couple this with your authorship and make money in multiple income streams.

Are you smelling what we are stepping in here, people? All of the above that I taught you so far is accomplished from your home.

Your home is the central core of your existence. You first become lean and mean and then turn your home into **passive and active income sources** by following the bouncing ball of the things I am teaching you.

The operative word here is HOME! By working from your home, you have more time to spend with your kids and family and think of the money you will save in day care.

By working from home you literally cut down on expenses – dry cleaning, wear and tear on your car, fuel bills, and more.

The benefits far outpace the negatives.

Chapter 7 – Advice & How To Information Products

I have been an Internet marketer since the net became public in 1989 and I have been selling informational products for about the same amount of time. Back then we only had email marketing to sell our stuff. Times have sure changed.

I am not going to get into everything that Internet marketing involves, otherwise this book would be the size of "War and Peace".

In Internet marketing there are two systems that dominate. They are affiliate marketing and cost-per-action marketing or CPA marketing. Both of these programs are where you sell other people's products. I don't do these; I don't sell products I have no control over.

I sell my products because I can control the quality, the quantity, the customer service and the fulfillment. Not because I am a control freak – I am – but because I have a saying I have used to guide me in business for quite a long time – **"A sale does not stop at the exchange of legal tender; it has only just begun."**

The most important part of a sale is customer service. My words mean nothing unless people put them into practice and since everybody is different when it comes to learning, I want to make myself available if they get stuck so they do it right the first time. In all of my books I give my personal email address and I really do respond to each one.

So, in this book I want to concentrate on Internet marketing where you are selling YOUR products and not other people's products.

Okay, in the book "Getting Paid For Everything You Do," it provides literally oodles of resources of tasks for a person to do and get paid for their daily work. It rocks and I have already said that this book should be in your personal library.

This book is for people that do not have a high skill level using a computer or have some difficulty learning new things. Unfortunately this is not my book but like I said, I was the adviser on the book and I know it inside and out so if you buy it and get stuck, write to me if you need help.

This book is perfect for senior citizens who did not grow up in the computer age and cannot find work because of their age.

I will tell you a little story to demonstrate how serious I am to customer service. A lady – Lori S - bought one of my books and wrote to me that she was having trouble implementing the programs. She lived in Los Angeles, which is about 6.5 hours from where I live. After numerous emails, I called her and she told me that she had four kids and her husband was laid off from his job. She was desperate to find income and had bought my book to do it. It turned out she had very little computer skills – could barely turn the computer on – and this was the reason for her problem.

Well, I grew up in Los Angeles – I am also a UCLA alumnus – so I decided to go pay Lori and her husband a visit and see how the old neighborhoods looked. WOW- did Los Angeles ever change but that is a good subject for another book. I have to tell you, the look on both of Lori and her husband's faces when I showed up armed with my laptop and air card was priceless. They simply could not believe that I would take my time and drive out to Los Angeles to help them.

Anyway, helping them was not easy because they both were practically brain dead using a computer so what I did was write out a simple tutorial on Step 1 then Step 2, etc and Lori was not to move on to the next step until she had mastered the first step, etc. this technique actually solved the problem because it forced Lori to concentrate step-by-step until she completed a task and got paid.

The reason why I bring up Lori and her husband is that I spoke to both of them just last week. She is up to $3,000/month and is no longer on food stamps or unemployment insurance. Her husband has quit looking for a job and is helping her with her new online business.

He even enrolled in the local city college for computer science courses and loving it.

It was nice helping them but I did get a chance to visit all of my old neighborhoods and stomping grounds. I simply cannot believe how the place had changed so dramatically. Santa Monica is now yuppie land with street markets and tons of tiny little bistros and coffee houses. I even got a chance to go to the beach and soak up some rays…that was really nice.

I stopped by all of the neighborhoods I lived in and came across one of the houses I lived in back in 1966. It was for sale so I called the realtor listed on the sign. My dad paid $38,500 for this house in 1966 and the sale price was now $750,000. OMG – I am convinced that everybody in California is smoking crack cocaine. How do young people begin their lives with real estate prices like that? Bloody, flipping amazing; but that is not all.

My family moved to California from New York in 1954. We first lived in San Diego but there were no jobs so we moved to Los Angeles and lived in Venice on the canals. Venice Canals was an attempt by a local developer to replicate the ones in Italy but was a dismal failure. Back then the canals were filthy and stagnant.

Anyway, I went back to see if the canals were still there and they were. The house I lived in was still there too but had been heavily updated and remodeled. It wasn't for sale but the one next door was so I called the realtor. Are you sitting down? The list price on the house was $2.2 million dollars. My dad paid $16,500 for the house next door in 1954. Is it any wonder why people are fleeing out of California? Even if I didn't own a car, I would walk out of that state just to get away from it…sheesh! Oh, and I almost forgot; the canals were still filthy and stagnant…amazing!

Okay enough of walking down memory lane…

Like I said, Internet marketing involves many aspects. To demonstrate, here is a list of my books just on Internet Marketing and Mobile Commerce, which is a sub-division of Internet marketing.

21st Century Marketing Genius
AWeber For Dummies
BlueprintCashPro
CashCodePro
Distraction Marketing
Effective Email Advertising
Fast TV EXPOSURE
In-Image Ads Marketing
Massive Traffic Generator
Pay Per Call Marketing
Pay Per View Advertising
PLR Cash Tactics
SEONemo ThenSEO
SEONemo NowSEO
SEONemo SoonSEO
Social Media Marketing
The Perfect Affiliate
The Postcarders
Traffic Jam
Traffic Media

Video Marketing
Web Traffic Systems
Word of Mouth Marketing (WOMM)
Mobile Commerce
It's All About Database
Mobile Commerce Blueprint
Mobile Text Voting
Selling Air
SMS Mobile Competitions
SMS Reverse Auction
To Boldly Go Mobile

You can find these books by going online to the ePubWealth.com Library Catalog:
EPW Library Catalog Online
http://www.epubwealth.com/wp-content/uploads/2013/07/Leland-benton-private-turbo.pdf

EPW Library Catalog Download
http://www.filefactory.com/f/562ef3ea1a054f0a

As you can see, Internet Marketing is nothing to sneeze at and involves many different aspects.

Out of all of the above I want to specifically talk about one really neat one called The Postcarders:

This is an automated postcard marketing program where you can sell your products using postcards BUT, everything is fully automated and you accomplish all of your marketing campaigns from your computer. You never touch or see the postcard. You design the postcard and offer on your computer. Then you provide a mailing list and the websites stated in the book will print the postcard, address the postcard, stamp it and mail it for you. Like I said, you never see or touch the postcard.

I love this program and to date I send out about 250,000 postcards each month. One thing I learned; there are people that refuse to use a computer. They don't own one; they do not have an email address…nothing. These are my best customers because they respond well to my offers. Here is another very weird thing that a gentleman I spoke to at a convention one day years ago taught me and it was a hard lesson to learn too. It is so weird; I am even having trouble putting it into words. Here is a postcard I designed for one of my products:

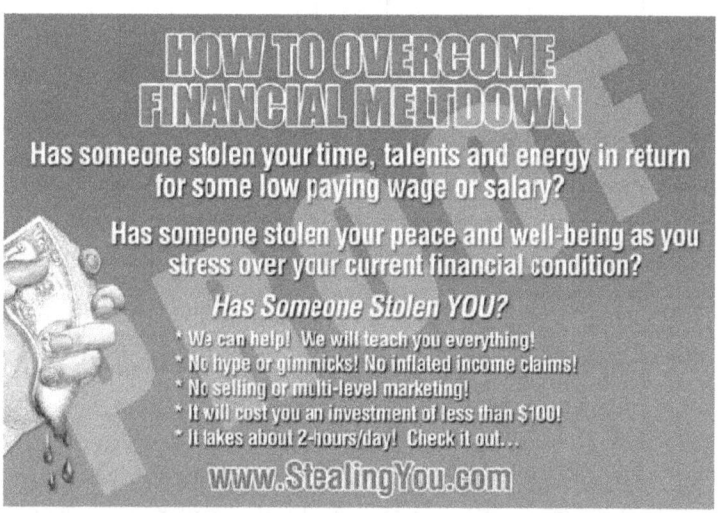

It was four colors on gloss enamel paper and did okay sales-wise until I showed it to the gentleman in question. BTW – this gentleman was labeled the "Postcard King" at the convention. He took one look at it and said I did it all wrong. He said it was too pretty and I needed to make it ugly. Then it would sell like hotcakes. To prove his point, he whipped out his laptop and said this is the postcard I should send:

How to overcome financial meltdown

Has someone stolen your time, talents and energy in return for some low paying wage or salary?

Has someone stolen your peace and well-being as you stress over your current financial condition?

Has Someone Stolen YOU?

We can help!

Candidly, I took one look at what he presented and then looked at him and said, "You have got to be kidding me!!!" And he wasn't; he told me to go and run the same campaign as I did with the pretty one substituting the ugly one and see the results for myself.

Reluctantly and I mean reluctantly, I did what he suggested and then almost fell over when the results came in. The ugly card out sold the pretty card like 5-to1. Bloody, flipping amazing! Don't even ask me why because I still, to this day, can't figure it out but the facts speak for themselves; when it comes to postcard marketing, ugly is better than pretty. That should be a bumper sticker!!!

Okay, in the next chapter I am going to list various opportunities available that you can easily implement. These opportunities I canister to be less meatier than the ones I have presented so far so study each one carefully to see if you have a passion for it.

Chapter 8 – Miscellaneous Niches That Rock!

1. Advice & How To: If you select writing books then the genre called Advice & How To without a doubt is the most lucrative genre and this is where I make the most money. To wit: here is a list of my books in this genre:

Advice/How To

Applied Mind Sciences
Addictions
Anatomy of Anxiety
A Weapon of Massive Consumption
A Woman Surrounds A Man
Blame Me Not
Body Language
Body Talk
Bouncing Back From Adversity to Success
Bully America
Cartoon Psychology

Chasing Shadows
Confessions of a Child Predator
Confessions of a Satanic Worshipper
Control Your Dreams
Fantasy Is Easy-Everything Is Perfect
Female Wolf Packs
Gender Differences in Advertising
How Do I Let Go?
How To Cope with Male Menopause
If It Is Broke; Fix It
I Have a Mind to Believe
I Know I Am But Who Are You
Interesting Facts About Left-Handed People
Living Alone
Love is the Way
Male-Female Realities
Man Up - The Decline and Fall of Manhood
Men & Women…attract or attack
Predictable Advertising
Questions
Satisfaction
Sexting & Text Flirting
Teen Idols
The Color of White
The Denial of Self
The Face of Anorexia
The Face Of Despair
The Greatest Fraud the World Has Ever Known
The Missing Link
The Other Side of Me
The Power of Concentration
The Power of Observation
The Science of Psychology EXPOSED

The Smack Report
The Vowel Movement
Too Late For Fruit; Too Soon For Flowers
What Is It About Yorkies
Will I Look Good In This
Wordz
You Can't or You Won't

You can find these books by going online to the ePubWealth.com Library Catalog:
EPW Library Catalog Online
http://www.epubwealth.com/wp-content/uploads/2013/07/Leland-benton-private-turbo.pdf

EPW Library Catalog Download
http://www.filefactory.com/f/562ef3ea1a054f0a

I have published a list of Amazon categories that demonstrate just how many genres and categories are available for you to write about. I couldn't include it in this book because it is 138-pages. Go here and download it for free:

http://tinyurl.com/epubwebinar2

If this doesn't get your creative juice flowing nothing will!

2. Health & Fitness: Another genre that is super lucrative is health and fitness. It is my second most profitable niche. To wit: here are some of the books I have published:

Health/Fitness/Alternative Medicine

Chelation Therapy
Drop Three Dress Sizes in 30-Days
Embarrassing Problems Fix - General Problems Vol 1
Embarrassing Problems Fix - Female Problems Vol 2
Embarrassing Problems Fix - Male Problems Vol 3
Energy Psychology
Getting Rid of Cellulite in 10-Days
If You Want to Get Big Eat a Pig
PhattyFat WheytLoss
The Complete Health System
The Pain Game
The Way to Flat Abs in 4-Weeks

You can find these books by going online to the ePubWealth.com Library Catalog:
EPW Library Catalog Online
http://www.epubwealth.com/wp-content/uploads/2013/07/Leland-benton-private-turbo.pdf

EPW Library Catalog Download
http://www.filefactory.com/f/562ef3ea1a054f0a

NOTE: if you write in multiple genres then use a pen name for each genre so as not to confuse your readers.

3. Investment/Income: Still another very lucrative genre is investment/income and this is my third most profitable niche.

Investment/Income

Applied Income Model
Getting Paid For EVERYTHING You Do!
How to Choose a Good Trading System
How To Marry Into Wealth
How To Monetize Social Trends
How To Retire Without Money
Money Is an Effect and Not a Cause
The Psychology of Sales
Triggers That Cause Buyers to Open Their Wallets

You can find these books by going online to the ePubWealth.com Library Catalog:
EPW Library Catalog Online
http://www.epubwealth.com/wp-content/uploads/2013/07/Leland-benton-private-turbo.pdf

EPW Library Catalog Download
http://www.filefactory.com/f/562ef3ea1a054f0a

4. DIY – Do it Yourself: There is one more very profitable niche that really rocks but I do not write in this niche because I am the most un-mechanical person on the planet. UL Laboratories could hire me to figure out how to break a product. If it's breakable you can bet I will find a way to do it. I am literally all thumbs when it comes to even the most simple mechanical; tasks. But just because I am a "lamer' when it comes to DIY doesn't means you are. This is a very lucrative niche and if you have a passion for doing anything with your hands then this is the niche for you.

When I buy Kindle books online – and I buy a ton of them – I usually buy books from the DIY niche. The lat book I bought was on woodworking and although I suck at woodworking I am determined to learn it. Thankfully I can do this in the privacy of my own home because if you were to watch me, you would probably end up soiling yourself with laughter...yeah I am that bad at it.

Thankfully, I have a brother-in-law that is very mechanical and he helps me around the hose. He knows I am partially retarded when it comes to anything mechanical and is patient with me. Also my garage is the paradise of tools. Amazing, eh? Here I am the most un-mechanical person on the planet yet I have every tool under the sun...and this was even after I downsized!!! My brother-in-law told my sister that I have more stuff in my garage then the local Ace Hardware Store and he isn't kidding.

I even have one of those four-wheel ATVs with a little trailer that I can pull behind it. I also bought the snow plow attachment and I really use this baby a lot. Where I live we get a lot of snow.

The ATV is also fun to take out into the woods. My Yorkie, Gage and I go whenever we get the opportunity and campout. I had a harrowing experience happen to me on one such campout. I built a little wire basket on the back of the ATV to hold my Yorkie and some camping stuff when we go out. On one excursion, Gage was barking up a storm and I turned to look at what he was barking at just in time to wave off a big red tail hawk that had his eye on making Gage his dinner. That scared me so I built a lid on the basket and keep a sharp eye out when Gage is with me. He doesn't go more than a couple of feet from me when we are in the woods.

4. Email Marketing: I began in the business, like I said previously, using Email Marketing as my primary marketing system mainly because in 1989 this is all we had. But email marketing has evolved into a very lucrative business model if done correctly. I simply cannot go into this marketing system in detail; there is too much to teach you. I wrote four books on the subject that teaches it to you step-by-step:

21st Century Marketing Genius
AWeber For Dummies
Effective Email Advertising
Distraction Marketing
Here is an inside tip: My "Distraction Marketing" book describes an email marketing technique that makes me gobs of money and when you read it you will see why. But first order the "Effective Email Advertising" book since it is the bible of email marketing. Once you learn email marketing then read the "Distraction Marketing" book.

You can find these books by going online to the ePubWealth.com Library Catalog:
EPW Library Catalog Online
http://www.epubwealth.com/wp-content/uploads/2013/07/Leland-benton-private-turbo.pdf

EPW Library Catalog Download
http://www.filefactory.com/f/562ef3ea1a054f0a

I Have a Special Gift for My Readers

I appreciate my readers for without them I am just another author attempting to make a difference. If my book has made a favorable impression please leave me an honest review. Thank you in advance for you participation.

My readers and I have in common a passion for the written word as well as the desire to learn and grow from books.

My special offer to you is a massive ebook library that I have compiled over the years. It contains hundreds of fiction and non-fiction ebooks in Adobe Acrobat PDF format as well as the Greek classics and old literary classics too.

In fact, this library is so massive to completely download the entire library will require over 5 GBs open on your desktop.

Use the link below and scan all of the ebooks in the library. You can select the ebooks you want individually or download the entire library.

The link below does not expire after a given time period so you are free to return for more books rather than clog your desktop. And feel free to give the link to your friends who enjoy reading too.

I thank you for reading my book and hope if you are pleased that you will leave me an honest review so that I can improve my work and or write books that appeal to your interests.

Okay, here is the link…

http://tinyurl.com/special-readers-promo

PS: If you wish to reach me personally for any reason you may simply write to mailto:support@epubwealth.com.

I answer all of my emails so rest assured I will respond.

Meet the Author

Dr. Leland Benton is Director of Applied Web Info, a holding company for ePubWealth.com, a leading ePublisher company based in Utah. With over 21,000 resellers in over 22-countries, ePubWealth.com is a leader in ePublishing, book promotion, and ebook marketing.

As the creator and author of "The ePubWealth Program," Leland teaches up-and-coming authors the ins-and-outs of today's ePublishing world. He has assisted hundreds of authors make it big in the ePublishing world.

Leland also created a series of external book promotion programs and teaches authors how to promote their books using external marketing sources.

Leland is also the Managing Director of Applied Mind Sciences, the company's mind research unit and Chief Forensics Investigator for the company's ForensicsNation unit. He is active in privacy rights through the company's PrivacyNations unit and is an expert in survival planning and disaster relief through the company's SurvivalNations unit.

Leland resides in Southern Utah.

Visit some of his websites
http://www.AddMeInNow.com
http://www.AppliedMindSciences.com
http://www.AppliedWebInfo.com
http://www.BookbuilderPLUS.com
http://www.BookJumping.com
http://www.EmailNations.com
http://www.EmbarrassingProblemsFix.com
http://www.ePubWealth.com
http://www.ForensicsNation.com
http://www.ForensicsNationStore.com
http://www.FreebiesNation.com
http://www.HealthFitnessWellnessNation.com
http://www.Neternatives.com
http://www.PrivacyNations.com
http://www.RetireWithoutMoney.org
http://www.SurvivalNations.com
http://www.TheBentonKitchen.com
http://www.Theolegions.org
http://www.VideoBookbuilder.com

www.ingramcontent.com/pod-product-compliance
Lightning Source LLC
Chambersburg PA
CBHW051818170526
45167CB00005B/2062